Visions of God

Written By

Cassie Marie

Table of Contents

"Through My Mother's Eyes"
"I AM" a Healer"

Calling all angels, sound the trumpet… time to wake them, time to bring them back to the love in Humanity. Happiness and prosperity are a right…YOUR birthright is a right given by God himself. We are in a spiritual war; the time has come to bring back the Kingdom! We have been misguided, programmed, and put to sleep so we can work for the government and the Ego of our society. We are under no ruler, yet they live and feast like Kings. While poverty spreads, children go hungry, and mothers cry. With all we have in this world of abundance, we are blind to see what our neighbors struggle with daily." Who are we to put a King over our Lord?" You wonder why we suffer and why our babies go hungry; message confirmation Archangel Michael 444. Everything on this earth was provided, free of charge, so it should be used in this way. Greed, power, and envy have caused a rise of Evil in this world. Now, lightworkers, Angels, and gifted beings will be finding you. You have been called to fight and awaken the army. We have been locked in a systematic prison to fund the hierarchy, and it is time to be free. Our children deserve to be free from oppression, pain, sadness, Anxiety, and Depression. Only WE can do that, and it must be an Army! We need you, we need God, and he has answered. The awakening is here, and he has risen! I see God because my mom has seen God. I

KNOW God because SHE knows God, and without her, I would never have gotten this far in my journey. I give full credit for this book to my mom, who never gave up on me and never doubted the potential I have inside of me. The fire, determination, and drive I possess came from her.

Children in schools are trained, programmed, and crafted for the workforce to ensure the future control and growth of our government. In school, they are graded, and the best ones get the best praise because they will one day bring the most money. We are raising our children, programming them to work for the government. Our priorities as a nation are backward.

Jeremiah 22:22

Revelations 22

ARCHANGEL MICHAEL PRESENTING:

REVELATIONS 12:7 – connection made through verse

"WE all have Evil in us for a purpose." Rise in battle, for now is the time to use the dragon you've trained. The war is upon us, take up arms, and gather the troops. All Angels 2 Kings 19:4, "I will enter this city and save it"

27JUL24 2351

In the name of the Father, Son, Angels, and Holy Spirit, I come to you so that you may better understand your ability as a person and child of God.

We are given and born with the gift of discernment. It is our world that shadows our vision and what we believe is true and what is false. The visions you see, feel and imagine were given to you through the Holy Spirit so that you should see what God has in store for you. This gift also gives us the ability to feel, love, and experience what others do.

The wisdom, strength, and courage to face the battles you fight daily come to you from within. You can channel that inner strength through meditation, Yoga, crafting, and spending time with nature. Whatever you do in life can be achieved by simply spending time with yourself and reconnecting with what you truly love about yourself. This brings you back (grounding) to oneness; therefore, back to God himself. You see, we are born with so much love, light, happiness, and joy. We are given that gift to be able to heal with love because it does cure all things. To know this, you must know God, and you must know yourself. In Jesus name we are healed, but we must feel this, live this, believe this, and spread this with nothing but love, light, pureness, and joy. Hope is in the future, and it is up to all of us to bring it to life. Love is within us because we are of God, and he lives in us all. There are no mistakes in life; everything you go through and everything you face is never for nothing. No matter what you face, just go right through it. Do not stop, do not look back, and do not question the lesson. Face each new day with a positive attitude and love in your heart. There will be bad times ahead, and some days will be worse than others. I am not here to sugarcoat anything. I am only here to tell you to have Faith in all you do, and nothing will fall to darkness. There will be no fear; there will be no pain. There will be no sickness. Heaven is here, and it is what you make of it. The choices you make in life determine the outcome of your life. No matter what you do, always take full advantage of the day you are given. Never fear for the future; it is not here, never mourn the past; it is no longer here. Stay present, stay grounded, and stay focused at all costs. The only way to succeed in life is to stay facing forward;" you cannot drive a car to your destination if you are driving in reverse."

The only way to save our world is to once again come together as a family, just the way God intended. When you are pure of toxins, greed, envy, and self-destruction. We are not black, we are not Asian, we are not Indian, we are not white. The color of our skin does not determine the outcome of our lives, and what we make of them. You are destined for greatness from the time you are placed in your mother's womb. To prosper, grow, and love just as God intended for himself, his son, and for all of us. We are damaging our own bodies, and we are damaging our own minds, and relationships with what we put into them. "Words cast spells, what you speak over life; it shall be." Time 1222.

I never doubted myself or what I was made of...until I made a mistake that would forever change my life. With Love and in Light Unity and Divinity, we come together.

I knew I wanted to heal the world, but I never knew how. There was always that still small voice in the back of my mind telling me to keep going. Even when the world was at its darkest, I kept going to spite it all. The ever-present light that flickered inside was something I longed for, that feeling of warmth, love, and light.

This healing will bring you to Jesus; he will be in you and all through you. Whatever you touch will turn to gold. All your dreams come to fruition. You will feel no more pain and no more sadness. I had to be made to feel the pain and sadness.

"When I come to you, I will bring witnesses."

You are missing yourself. Think about what you really love doing for you and make it a priority. It is important to make sure time is spent doing what you really love about yourself. The very things that you love most about yourself and what makes you unique are the exact things that make all those around you love you that same way. Being authentic and genuine is a gift you give yourself. The only true person who knows you better than anyone is you. To be one with yourself, you must be one with God. To accomplish that, everything around you needs to be controlled. You must control who, what, when, and where always. Who will be there? Is there a crowd? Will I feel comfortable? All of those are very logical ways of thinking when deciding to go out or stay in. That is completely your right to do so. This is giving yourself control over who or what sends negative energy and darkness your way. We are all made of energy, and we truly have a vibrational pattern and rhythm; hence the heartbeat you feel and hear on the outside but only feel on the inside. When our minds and Chakras are aligned, our mood and vibration are in order, and we can see things for what they truly are. All the smoke clears; to be one in God is to be one in yourself. Grounding is an important part of well-being and abundance due to not only the healing benefits you get, but it brings us back to right now. We are still part of this Universe, which means we float. On the days you feel like your head is in the clouds, create something. On the days you feel out of your mind or body, you really need to spend time with nature and take in every benefit of the living earth. We are provided all the natural resources to survive, and completely free of Charge. We are the ones who decided to put it on the shelf, and we are the ones who put a price on things we need. Everything becomes so clouded by the expectations and demands of everyday life that we get caught in the rush. We are in constant competition with ourselves and each other. Nobody was sent here to feel less than anything or anyone. That is self-inflicted and contagious. The longer you allow negative thoughts and emotions to live in your head, the more power you give them. You can spend an eternity chasing away demons that haunt you, but you can never completely get rid of them until you decide to take the time necessary for healing your mind and soul, which, in return, your body follows.

Mark 1236: "For <u>Da'-vid himself and said by the Holy Ghost.</u> Mark 1238 And he said unto them in his doctrine, "Beware of the scribes, which love to go in long clothing and love situations in the marketplaces," Beware of the people who cover up who they really are. The ones who wear dark clothing and walk around in a cloak (spiritually) to blind you to your true vision and purpose in life. You need to be cautious of those around you, and God has given you the ability to see people for exactly who they are. The darkness they possess will always come to light.

Because you are of love and light, the darkness is attracted to you like a moth to the flame, and darkness is drawn by light. The darkness from within is very scary and consumes all that it crosses. For that reason, make sure to stay away from others on days you don't feel yourself in control of your emotions or thoughts. That is where things attach to each other. Everyone is an Empath; that gift they call empathy. Finding the lining is harder on those days because we need our loved ones the most for support, but it is called "emotional support" because you give that gift to those who need it most. Even more so when those people that you need it from are family. Eventually all your good emotions and love are exhausted, so you need it back in return. It gets tricky then because we go back to those who we loved so purely during their need, expecting the same feeling and healing in return. Time and emotions are expensive; be very wary of who you spend it on and with. Those people determine where your soul goes and how it grows. Not being able to get that back when you need it the most is enough to take you off this planet. The rejection and pain of not having that connection or healing when you need it the most is what kills people. It takes on Hell of a person to come back from that one. You must fight tooth and nail for yourself, and it looks very much like mental illness. That diagnosis is a label that will keep you in a mental prison because it defines who you are in your own mind. It must be true because the doctor says so, right? But it's your body that plainly says, "Hey, my mind is sick, and it needs healing. Family ties and bonds are the hardest yet most detrimental to your health. Some bonds are so strong that you literally cannot function without one another. Those attacks on your spirit and soul come from the darkness hiding in the shadows. Any drama and old wounds you do not address and heal from resurface and repeat until you finally take the time to deal with it, and process completely. Throughout our lives, we will heal more from our own family members than people we don't even know.

The moment you enter this world, you are born dying. You are instantly put in a state of growth and death at the very same time. The definition of death is the permanent ending of vital processes in a cell or tissue, which is exactly what we are made of. If you are not growing and nourishing your mind or soul, then you are dying. When your mind is starved of the nutrients and environment it needs, it turns internally. Your organs work like a train if you really think about it. A train will go full force, completely unstoppable and dangerous to anything that crosses its path. That very same train will completely derail if one part of it stops working with the rest. First, the train will burn extra fuel and energy, making up for what it needs but it does not have to function at full force. In return, the strong parts of the train wear down to almost nothing. Suppose the conductor (Mind) is responsible for maintaining the train (Body). To keep his train running, it will need fuel (Food for the mind and soul), maintenance (Mind and Body), and time off to rest (Soul). "Greater is he that lives inside of me."

Everyone dies, but not everyone lives. Being alive does not mean you are living. It only means that you are breathing. To live is to love and laugh. After a lifetime of trauma and wondering why me…I finally see. Nothing was ever sent to hurt me; it was sent to teach me how to fight. How to come back from the dead, and how to always see the best in others no matter what I was dealing with. Because of this, God granted me the gift of discernment, the vision to see real intentions, and the healing path others need to find him.

You will lose people in your life. Some of the most important ones will turn on you. This transformation is intense and as fast as you make it. The more you put into learning yourself, the more people think you are insane. That whole people-pleasing bubble has burst into thin air. This ride is a challenge about earning your stripes. God gives the toughest battles to his strongest warriors. Your Spiritual Journey will take you through many timelines, dimensions, and realms. Started from the bottom now I'm here… KEEP CLIMBING. It's God at the end of the tunnel, and he is waiting for you. In Jesus's name. Amen.

Our journey begins and ends with God, and he is the Alpha and Omega. Your destiny is decided before you leave his hands. We are in the time of Revelations. Your true calling has been with you, the visions, the thoughts, things you see and feel…. was your Holy

Ghost guiding you the whole time. He allowed you to see the good in people so that you would be ready for this war! Now is the time to pull everything together and head into the battlefields. CALLING ALL ANGELS- your time is here. It is a time of reckoning, awakening, coming together, and accepting love to heal our world. We are hurting, so God is sending his son back through each one of us." For God so loved the world, he gave his only begotten son" John 3:16 WE are the sons, and we are the daughters. Adam and Eve were the first so they might be used as a vessel and brought life through human form. We are all created in his image. Not black, white, or Hispanic, WE ARE ONE. Come together and heal this world, or suffer the wrath. This war has been on for years. We are all blinded by democracy and governmental programming and cannot see. Your loved ones are always with you, guiding you through the troubles of life, and will give you the gift of sight to have them and hold them for eternity. They are not gone!

Mark 3:16 in the Bible says, "He appointed the twelve. We are not our bodies on this earth, and we are a soul in a body. And that body will deteriorate if it is not fed properly. This requires spiritual nourishment, physical, and mental. One does not function without the other, same with the organs in your body. We are all connected, and we are all aligned. We live through many timelines, but we forget due to mainstream programming and poisoning... Our government is ALLOWING poisonous toxins in our food so that we may be heavy and weighed down. To reach this level of knowing, there is a required fast and life change so the body and mind can heal from the lifetime of damage caused. We are the healers. You do not need a doctor to tell you what is happening to your body. Nobody knows you the way you do. Pray about it, and ask God… he will send the cure. But we are not all awake yet because we are ADDICTED to these things… money, power, greed, ego, toxins, bad habits. Because of that addiction, we are further and further from God's love. We do not FEEL it because we are numbed by the world we are in. To raise this nation and this world, We must purge ALL evil, darkness, and toxins to Ascend into our Highest Power and potential. This is my gift to you. I hope it will serve as a guiding light on your journey home…with love always

~Camarie~

MESSENGER

Vision received 27JUN2024:

I am a messenger for God through visions received while channeling my mother. These signs come through visual, audio, songs, numbers, animals, and many other ways. People call me crazy because they cannot see what I do. I know the power within myself, and I am very capable of saving this world with the love and light passing through me given by God above. What I get to experience is an absolutely amazing ride full of love and healing for others who miss family. I will continue telling my stories; the right person will hear it, and their life will be forever changed. Jesus saved me, and because of that, I have a purpose to serve the Lord. He gives me the vision to see things for what they really are. I see and feel the guilt, pain, and evil of this whole world. It makes my body sick to think our world has gotten to this current point. God is speaking to everyone. Jesus was a visionary and the son of God…as are we. Open your heart and mind before this world is too far gone. This life was not meant to be lived in struggle.

This is something I hope and pray my family and friends awaken in time to enjoy this within me. I have the gift of visions, feeling, healing, and knowing because I know God, and I know Jesus. The Holy Ghost lives in me. I went through many struggles to reach this point, but I will not give up on myself because you are not comfortable with my demons. Mine have been set free through this journey, and that is where I found them. We cannot see or feel them because we are blind to the possibility. Have faith in yourself and in Love, and you will find them all.

My healing journey has been incredible, frightening, lonely, and freeing. Your new life is just around the corner. I found my way, and I can light yours… whenever you are ready, I will guide you there. I have this ability to see beyond the veil, so my vision is clear. God is real; the time is now, and we are the only ones who can save us. God has sent his angels to earth as infants. We are all angels born in human form. Heaven is already here, and we are the warriors!

*~ **We all have to let our light shine.***

~~Dedicated to my mom and guardian, Angel Jackie Harwood~ for the gift of sight, faith, courage, strength, and wisdom used in this book.

Your loved ones are not gone. You just can't see them until you know Jesus Christ. When you accept him and the holy ghost into your mind body and soul. You will be walking in heaven with them all right here from this earth.

SPIRITUAL LEVELS

The Rebirth

1. WITH GOD
2. BIRTH ASSIGNMENT AND REBIRTH
3. LIFE LEARNING AND LESSONS
4. LOSE YOURSELF AND EXPECTATIONS OF LIFE
5. ROCK BOTTOM
6. LIFE ACCEPTANCE
7. THE CLIMB
8. THE FALL
9. THE CLIMB
10. THE RISE

Cassie, AKA Camarie (actual reading)

28JUL24   1908 Music is your Muse

"She's been through the fire"- Jen

Color Purple

Hummingbird in the window*

Always has a hard time falling asleep- loves babies, love notes, and everyone (pure of heart full of love and light)

*Always make time for yourself and healing. Be easy on yourself, and you are healing. It will get worse before it gets better. There will be days you do not recognize yourself, some days you will not want to face the world. On those days, be kind to yourself. Find grace and peace in every storm.

*If I would have known- Make the best of the life you have, feel love, joy, and happiness. Your journey is about acceptance and believing. You have an angel guiding your every move. This person misses you very much; you think of them often and wish they could see you now. I feel maybe they present to you, and you feel them at that very moment.

-You are more than enough- The beauty in your eyes and goodness in your heart. You are here for a reason. Please believe you are more than enough and more than capable. Miracles happen every day; don't waste one minute doubting. Even on your hardest day, there's wind on your back, holding you steady on your course. Nothing will keep you from having all you desire in life as long as you keep believing you are more than enough.

*Bleeding Love- Time starts to pass before you know it. All the love you put out should be returned 10-fold. Stop giving your energy, time, and love to those who drain you. Old wounds should never bleed. The goal is to keep you from falling off track; stay one in your mind, body, and soul. Protect yourself by cutting unnecessary ties to people, places, and things that no longer serve your higher purpose. Negative emotions are a weapon, fear, anger, stress, and depression are labeled as a disease. They are only DIS- eases (uncomfortable symptoms)

    *Take Me There- Came to you with a broken faith. Would you take the wheel if I lose control? Your husband is your armor and strength. Even on days you want to give up, he is there. Communication is key. Always have a safe space for emotions and feelings. At times, you will feel like you are dying.

Your body is healing, detoxing, and renewing. Therefore, you will experience a spiritual death to be reborn. I will lead you through this and guide you all the way. Please have faith, the journey will be dark, it will be scary, and it will be love, it will be joy. Your husband will need to be your rock, your armor, your dragon, and your protector. He was sent to you by God for this very moment…. Jennifer, welcome to your awakening and welcome home, love.

*Lose Control- (EGO) You will battle your mind, and demons of your past, present, and future. You will battle the world. At times, you will feel insane, at times, your family will think you are losing it. Angels will appear in perfect time, and God, Jesus himself, will be in and all around you and your home. Forget society's standards of what is expected/ what is explainable/ and what is logical. We are in a world full of wonders, and soon, you will meet them and go there. We are amazed by the Universe. Yet, at the same time, part of that very same wonder. God, Universe, and Source have you in their arms.DO NOT BE AFRAID

*Little bit better- Going through the darkness will get better. I am telling you how to die and come back into consciousness. This is very crucial in your journey and requires focus, dedication, and intentions. This will be forever; you will own the darkness. You will never fall susceptible to illness or disease once you return with your light. To obtain it, we go to our inner self.

This includes past pains, regrets, doubts, and insecurities. This is your healing plan.

*Lost Boys- Believe in him and believe in yourself. Together, he will carry you to your destiny. The family will be your loving shield and comfort. Use physical contact and deep breathing exercises to pull love, life, and healing into your body. Let it fill your lungs every time. Your prescription from today forward is LOVE LOVE LOVE. And lots of it! Run, Run, lost boy. Be young, be free, and fill your days with memories. Always be pure in your heart and free of negativity.

*Pray- Waking up but wishing that you don't is something you never want to know. Anything you put out in the Universe will return in abundance. I pray you never know guilt. It consumes your soul.

*Someone you loved equals the day bleeds into nightfall. You are not here to help me through it… Your angel is with you to guide you, and there are times she will carry you without you asking. Always allow her to cover you in her wings with her loving warmth, light, and glow. She is your (motherly type) …Grandma, maybe. She is soft and gentle, loving and kind. Her hugs are so warm and comforting. Feel that embrace when you need her, and she will be there. She is with you always. She loves you so much and wishes you happiness and joy.

*Only Love Can Hurt Like This- Her passing was damaging to your spirit; she knows that and wants your healing. She has never left your side.

*Therapy- Anytime you need her, feel her in your heart, and at that time, you will be one. The love you feel is hers. You can't lose her.

You are exactly who I've been waiting for.

Red

Ruby

Purple

Blue

Hummingbird

Jade for wellness

Ballerina

Message sent, received, and ended 28JUL24 2115

28JUL24 2120 – "Food for healing and water for life" ~end reading

References:
The Holy Bible

Authorized King James Version

With words of Christ in Red

Holman Bible Publishers

Nashville, TN

<u>DR, SEBI TREATMENT BOOK</u>

By: Aniys Hendry

RISE OF A LIGHTWORKER

By: Will Sibley

Accreditations:

Psychology Graduate

Usui Reiki Master

Retired Healthcare Worker